MY BOOK OF
POETRY
Dedications

MY BOOK OF POETRY
Dedications

JENEIL YOUNG

iUniverse, Inc.
Bloomington

MY BOOK OF POETRY DEDICATIONS

iUniverse books may be ordered through booksellers or by contacting:

iUniverse
1663 Liberty Drive
Bloomington, IN 47403
www.iuniverse.com
1-800-Authors (1-800-288-4677)

ISBN: 978-1-4759-8109-4 (sc)
ISBN: 978-1-4759-8110-0 (ebk)

Printed in the United States of America

iUniverse rev. date: 03/09/2013

THIS BOOK IS

DEDICATED

TO THE THREE MOST

IMPORTANT MEN IN MY LIFE

FIRST TO GOD FOR INSTILLING

THIS GIFT IN ME AND FOR GUIDING

ME THROUGH IT TO THE END.

SECOND TO MY FATHER TO FOLLOW

IN HIS FOOTSTEPS TO WRITING A BOOK

OF POETRY AS HE HAD THAT HAS CARRIED

INTO A SECOND GENERATION.

THIRD TO MY HUSBAND FOR ALWAYS

BELIEVING AND INCOURAGING ME TO FOLLOW

THROUGH WITH THIS DREAM OF MINE AND

FOR HIS LOVE AND STRENGTH TO CARRY ME

THROUGH TO FINISHING THIS BOOK.

MY BOOK OF

POETRY

DEDICATIONS

IS A REFLECTION UPON MY FEELINGS

OF THOSE WHOM HAS TOUCHED MY LIFE.

THESE ARE MY PERSONAL FEELINGS

TO HONOR THOSE WHOM I LOVE, I MISS,

AND I CHERISH THAT I WILL FOREVER

CARRY IN MY HEART

AND TO THOSE

WHOM HAVE FOREVER IMPACTED MY

LIFE IN SO MANY DIFFERENT WAYS.

FOR THE LOVE, THE HOPE, AND THE DREAMS

OF THE PAST, THE PRESANT AND THE FUTURE

FROM THE PEN OF IT'S AUTHOR.

CONTENTS

A DEVINE PAIR YOU ARE

Two people so special as you are,
Are wrapped around my heart with delicate lace.
And each time I look into your face: I see the beauty, I feel the grace.
You have soothed my soul with such peace and kindness and
In my heart is where they'll find us.

You both have shown me a love that only I can define as
Heavenly sent a master piece God has lent us of his finest mint.
So as I close this poem and have my final say.
I want the two of you to know I love you both and
It will always be this way.
As I thank God for you both in so many different ways.

BY:JESY

3-23-2012

 A POEM FOR KAYLA

I heard on the news today of
A young girls life taken away
That shattered a mothers heart in two
And her fathers heart too.
So many lives affected.
Those whom knew her,
Those whom didn't; such as I
God only knows why.

My heart goes out to her friend
Whom was with her that tragic day.
And to all of her family and friends.
My prayers are with you all
As the shock and sadness begins to fall.
May God carry each one of you
In your hours of sorrow, I'll pray for you.
For you did not die in vain
And in our hearts your memory remains.

BY:JESY
(JENEIL E. SPARKS-YOUNG)
6-24-2012

# A SISTER'S LOVE

You will never know the depths of love;
 I have for you.
Because you have down syndrome.
You are my brother and I've raised you like a mother;
Since momma died.
God; now I know how hard she tried.

It breaks my heart in two
When people make fun of you and
In your world I know you'll never understand
But in my heart I do and the tears I cry are for you.
A forever childish like mind
Encountering the harshness of man kind.

And in my world I thought I was the one doing
All the teaching to you but
You have taught me so many things too.
How special I feel to have a brother like you
A sisters love so deep, so true.

BY:JESY

5-2-2012

AMAZING LOVE

As a child of Gods,
I kneel at the alter and give all of me to you.
I ask for forgiveness for the things I do
And you heal me with the power in you.

I can feel your amazing love coming over my soul
Caught up in emotions out of control.
As I stand in the presence of you.

Then the sensations of a lasting feeling
Of your amazing love.
Intertwines my heart and mind and
Showers me with soothing comfort
of a power of love to heal the soul.

There is no other love in this world
That could ever compare.
As I am in the presence of you.
Wrapped around my soul
This amazing love to carry me through
Until the day I am with you.

BY:JESY

11-25-2012

BEST FRIEND'S

There's a special kind of friendship,
We both share
That stems through the years,
We hold so dear.
It all started a long time ago,
Between you and me.
A friendship that has lasted for years;
And a bond we have shared.
It's all about being there for each other
Or reaching out a helping hand.
Together we found a special friend;
In each other.

BY:JESY

# BOUNDARIES

Why does it not surprise me
When I get close to you
You walk away
When I try so hard to make you feel special
You push me away
I know you love me (I hope it's true)
But sometime you make me wonder
What's inside of you.

How can you make me feel
When you show me no emotions revealed
What have I done to you
To leave my heart in limbo like you do
Why is it so hard for you
To make me feel what I want too with you
I want to know who hurt you so deep
To make you feel you should treat
A heart so loving true as mine is to you.
Left so alone here with & without you.

Life is too short to hurt me anymore
The tears I cry are for me.
And when you can come back to me
Without these boundaries
Then my heart will feel alive again.
Don't take this love for granted
For it only comes once in a lifetime
Be happy someone loves you the way I do.
For in an instant it could all be gone.

BY:JESY

7-30-2012

DADDY'S LITTLE GIRL

I remember a time in my life when
Nothing else mattered but the love you gave me.
The strong arms you wrapped around me that
Protected me from the harm this world could bring
A time when all I wanted to do was
Play with my dolly and
Pretend I was a princess in a fairy tale land.

A time when I grew older and realized that
Times were not always easy and
When you put your dreams on hold just
So we could grow up as a family and
A time when you were growing tired and
A time when you got sick and
Left this world far too soon or at least for me.

I remember a time when I used to be
Daddy's little girl and
Wish just one more time that
I could Play the role of a princess in your eyes

BY:JESY

12-8-2011

DADDY'S WEEPING CRY'S

In the quietness of the night
As I lay in my bed
I can hear your weeping cry's.

Lost in the confusion
Of your world torn apart
Left to pick up the pieces of a broken heart.

The tears that I cry are not only for me
But also for the whole family
When momma died.

The memories that's haunted me
Are the ones of you daddy
Piercing the future without her
We thought you'd never get through.

Now looking back upon those days of years ago
The echo's of daddy's weeping cry's
I've never seem to let go.

31 years together they were
When momma died
And 19 years of echo's I have cried.

BY JESY

11-12-2012

ECHO'S

I hardly ever see you anymore and
We haven't spoken in a long time.
I remember when I used to call you
my little googenhime.
You've grown older now and have a
Family of your own but in my mind
the echo's of your voice still roams.

If I could take away the years that
Has left a lonely space in my heart
Then I would.
I miss the late night conversations and
The anticipation of hearing from you.

Don't worry I'll be fine just
When ever you get the time
We'll get together again.
For you are not only my niece your
My best friend.
So remember I'm always proud of you
No matter what you do and
Most of all I'll forever love you.

BY:JESY
3-6-2012

FOREVER I DO

There stands the two pine trees
We got married between.
Vows we made that day still holds true and
I'm still in love with you.
It will be 8 years this year and I still want you dear
I don't want to see me without you.

I hold in my heart
A love that each day feels brand new and
It's all because of you I feel the way I do.
A love like no other and I'll share it all with you.
Forever I do, forever with you.

BY:JESY
1-18-2012

FOREVER MY FRIEND

Unlike the world we see, two people you and me
See the world differently.
But in our hearts we have found a friendship so profound
As we have shared emotions unwound.

For in this life you see your friendship means so much to me.
For your kindness allows my heart to be free and
I want you to know I'm grateful to you for
All the things you do that causes my heart to shine upon you.

For in my mind you will always be the one friend to me
The special one you see.
Forever remember me when this life should come to an end
For I will tell the angels about you; my friend.

BY:JESY
(JENEIL E. SPARKS, YOUNG)
8-10-2012

FRIEND OF MINE
PLEASE COME HOME

I see the gray in your hair and an empty stare
That didn't used to be there and
A sadness I've never seen that is concerning me.
You've been a friend of mine since we were little girls.
Close as two friends could be, we are almost like sisters.

Years have passed us by and close we still are.
We've been through many things together and
In my heart I'll love you forever.
But I've been noticing a change in you that worry's me.

If only you could see the side of you I see and
Take it up with God to free you and relieve you
So you can let it go to free your soul of a deep depression:
A world you've come to know.
God how I miss the woman I used to know.
Friend of mine please come home
You've been gone far too long.

BY:JESY

3-29-2012

 # "GODS GREATEST GIFTS"

God gave his only son:
To forgive us for what we've done.
A miracle for all of us to see.
A love that will stretch through eternity.
All he asks from us is to believe in him.
Give our heart and soul and be born again.
Trust and bring peace unto the lord
And then he will give us our reward.
The ten commandments were written in stone.
Do unto it and the light will be shone.
Then Gods greatest gifts will not be unknown.
For you will reap the seeds you have sown.

BY:JESY

GONE BUT NEVER FORGOTTEN

You lived your life full of goodness
Within the things you've done.
Filled us full of love when we were apart
For the kindness that was in your heart.
This young life that had future plans
that was taken from us by another's hands.

We can not bring you back to us I know this is true
for me the pain still runs so deep; of the loss of you.
How can this be justice when there was none
And this sadness that will forever carry on.

And 15 years you lived your life here on earth
Of your kindness since your birth.
Instilled in you a precious gift of a love to give
To everyone around you; we'll forever relive.

The anger still lies within
for a justice that should have been.
I can not change that I know
It's just something that God only knows.

2 years ago we said our goodbyes at your grave side
But in my heart a love so deep within
Will never be forgotten; for your my nephew, my friend.

BY;JESY
(JENEIL E. SPARKS-YOUNG)
10-22-2012

HAPPY BIRTHDAY MY SON

My heart has been breaking
since you've passed away.
My love for you will never fade away
from my mind, From my heart
its been there from the start.
Each and every day I feel the same way.
I miss you son.

The years we shared together are now
treasured memories for me.
For in my heart and mind.
You: this son of mine.
I'll never forget your face and
No one will ever take your place.
Happy birthday my son
Daddy will always love you.

BY:JESY

5-3-2012

HAVE YOU EVER?

Have you ever seen the ocean?
Or had a notion—to fall in love.
Ever seen the sun rise?
Or gave someone a warm surprise.

Have you ever been in love?
Or seen a turtle dove
Ever held a wedding band?
Or reached out a helping hand.

Have you ever helped a friend?
Or ever looked deep within.
Ever had struggles and strife's?
Or ever changed someone's life.

Have you ever been kind
To someone's heart or mind?
Ever gone out of your way
To lift someone's spirit up on any givin day.

And if you have ever done these things
May one of Gods angels spread her wings
Surround you with many wonderful things
And protect you in your dreams.

BY:JESY
10-25-2012

HE TOUCHED ME

It must have been in the words
That were spoken.
That moved me and soothed me.
That made me begin to think that
Things were starting to look up.
A little bit of faith began to
Grow inside my soul.

I remember hearing the preacher say
Believe and things will come,
Will come your way.
A soulful man, rich with truth
Speaking to the elderly clear
Down to the youth.
It was in a heavenly spirit his
Message was delivered in.
That wrapped my soul around
His words then I began to believe again.

He touched me with his words and
His message was clear.
I was free from sin, I was free from fear.
I knew then that God would always
Surround me with his love.
He touched me with a message sent
From heaven above.

BY:JESY
1-26-2012

HER ?

Sometimes we didn't get along
Reasons are unknown to me.
Unless it was the clashing of
Our opinions that differs her from me.
We lived in the same household but
We were worlds apart.
Even still she has a special place in my heart.

I wished for the closeness we never
Seemed to have together but
No matter what I'll still love her forever.
She will always be apart of me.
This much is true you see.
You know who you are and This I won't explain.
I'll just say she's her ? A woman with no name.

BY:JESY

1-20-2012

HONEY IT IS YOU

A candle light dinner for two
A story about me and you.
I've loved you from the start
Because of the way you've touched my heart.
With your loving ways toward me
That no one else sees.

Honey it is you that moves me
Awakens my soul and soothes me.
Your kindness is so sweet
Even to those you meet.
You believe in me; like I do you
Two hearts forever true.

Honey it is you that I love
We'll be together like two turtle doves.
I'll thank God for this love so right
As I lay next to you tonight.
I'll count my blessings one, two, three . . .
As I say goodnight to you honey.

BY:JESY

9-30-2012

I WOULD

If I had wings,
I would fly like a butterfly high into the sky
until I saw the stairs to heaven.
I would walk up the stairs and
Ask the Man at the gate if he would get you for me
Just so I could see you one more time.

I would ask you if you were ok and
Tell you I love you and I miss you more than
you'll ever know.
I would tell you everyone is fine and
They send their love too then
I would hug you and softly whisper to you goodbye.

I would turn around and thank the man at the gate and
blow you a kiss and walk down Those stairs and
Turn back into a butterfly.
I would fly back down to earth and
turn back Into me and tell myself;
God that felt so good just to see you one more time.

BY: JESY

11-11-11

 # IN MY FATHERS FOOTSTEPS

Memories of a household seems to unfold in my mind.
Of a time when children were laughing and playing
And everyone was saying I'd grow up just like you
And follow in my fathers footsteps of
Writing these poems like I do.
Father it was because of you.

You have inspired me deep down inside my soul.
It has opened up this side of me and set my memories free
To tell stories of our family and reflections of my life
Of the struggles and the strife's.
I'm proud to live my life in my fathers footsteps.

BY:JESY

3-1-2012

IN THE ARMS OF AN ANGEL

Scattered all around the house
Was white feathers on the floor.
She couldn't figure out where
They had come from
So she opened the door
And went about her day.

Driving down the highway
On this cold stormy day.
She passed an old woman holding
A sign saying be careful along the way.
She arrived at work A little late that day
And on the ground laid
A single white feather at her feet.

It was closing time

And she was heading home.

When a semi skidded off the road

And crashed into a ditch.

She stopped and jumped out of

Her car ran and dragged the man out

And held him in her arms.

As the truck blew up

Her wings spread out and covered the man

And protected him.

Then the man realized he was in

The arms of an angel.

BY:JESY

4-14-2012

IN THE LIGHT OF YOUR LOVE

It is the beauty of your face
That takes my mind to a special place
And my heart is in awe of you.

Tangled in a web for the thoughts I have
That carry's me through the power in you
To turn my world upside down.

Illusions in our conversations
That causes confusion in my mind
And a feeling of being lost without you.

Torn between family and friends
And me falling in love with you
That tares my world in two.

Then I make up my mind
And I focus only on you
Caught up in a world for two.

Then the world outside disappears
And I give all of me to you
As I stand in the light of your love.

BY:JESY

10-30-2012

IT MUST HAVE BEEN

The way you looked at me must have
Sparked the fire in my mind.
To make me think we'd be together for a long time.
And then you leaned in and Softly whispered in my ear
That made me want to be with you for years
Then you reached out and took my hand
That made me want you as my husband.
Then you leaned in and Pressed your lips to mine
That made me feel this love could last a lifetime.
You took the fire and lit the flame to
The candle of my soul and
Once again made me feel whole and
I just wanted you to know
I love you soo . . . .

BY:JESY

1-2-2012

LOVE FOUND ME

All of my life I've givin love away to
Everyone around me.
I held in my heart a special kind of love
I'd give when he found me.
A bond, a love, a trust of faithfulness
Would always surround me.
Then one day fate had its way and
Love found me.

I never dreamed I'd find someone like you
Everything I'd wished for
Had finally came true.
God had answered my prayers the day
We found each other and
Blessed us with a love like no others.

A work of art only god could have made
This wonderful man I had longed for and craved.
Its been 18 years this year and I still want you dear.
Fate got it right as I lay next to him each night.
As you look down and see
Thank you God love found me.

BY:JESY

1-21-2012

LOVING HANDS

In the universe of my soul
I'll find you there
With a bounty of angels
Dancing in the air.
With a story to be told of my
Heavenly fathers plan.
I behold a story
Of a mothers loving hands.

Touched with the beauty
Of a life Within
This new life will now begin.
Brought to her a new found love
A gift sent from heaven above.
A baby; she did give birth too
That changed her life
and made it brand new.

She Held her in her arms so tenderly
And she thought how beautiful
She is to me.
As the tears of happiness
Was rolling down her cheek.
 no words could she speak.
She checked her fingers and toes
All was there
as she buttoned up her clothes.
She Held her baby to her chest
And thought to herself
this life is the best.

BY:JESY

12-11-2011

MEMORIES OF A LIFETIME

It seems like just yesterday that you moved away.
The memories of us are still fresh in my mind.
There memories of a lifetime.

I still see us laughing and playing and
The merry-go going around.
How I miss those days and your silly ways.
You had gone away to another place
I've searched many people hoping to see your face.

And all the time we have shared I have stored in my mind.
You've left me here with memories of a lifetime.
Thank you my friend maybe one day we'll see each other again.

BY:JESY
6-25-2012

MY CHILDHOOD FRIEND

Remembering things and distance dreams are
Coming to my mind of yester year they are here
And flooding through is the memory of you and
All the things we used to do.

Just like then my heart remembers when
We used to laugh and play
Then one day heaven became your home and
I felt all alone.
My heart was left to mend
How I've missed you my childhood friend.

And as the years have passed me by
In my heart your memory has stayed alive.
Unless it's because I didn't want to say goodbye.
And maybe on the other side I'll see you again
I'll forever remember you my childhood friend.

BY:JESY
8-8-2012

MY GUIDING LIGHT

In the midst of the night
I see your glowing light
Leading me to you
And from afar I can see
You reaching out your light to me
Guiding me closer to you.

And in the shadows of the trees
I see the beast trying to come between
Me reaching my dreams and goals at hand.
I resist the temptation of giving up on you
From the struggles I have gone through.

Now I stand before you
In the height of your light
Grasped firmly as my future looks so bright.
I'll soar to the sky with my goals so high.
For this journey was a hard fight
Because I never gave up on you my guiding light.

BY:JESY

10-27-2012

NATURES FURY

Living in a world of confusion
And illusions running wild in my mind.
Devastation all around on the ground
From the aftermath of hurricane sandy.

Power outages and a neighborhood brought to ashes
That was a terrifying scene.
For there was power within this storm
So angry, so mean.

The death toll continues to rise
As the water subsides
In the places hit so hard by the super storm.

And as another storm approaches to bring
Insult to injury and cold weather on its way
My prayers are with you all through these troublesome days.

BY:JESY
11-5-2012

NO MORE TO GIVE

As I have begun to think of you again today
And the haunting memories that won't go away.
I try to fight them but they always seem to win
Then this sadness begins to creep in.
My feelings start to ache, then my tears begin to flow
I hear a voice say he's gone; I whisper I know.

Your picture still hangs on my wall just like it always did.
And in my mind your memory; I'll forever relive.
The love I've had for you has never ended for me
Because he was my nephew; you see.

I know nothing can bring you back to us
For it must have been your time to go
You had so much life left to live
God said you have no more to give
And heaven is now your home
As our hearts were left here without you; so alone.

BY:JESY
4-4-2012

ONCE AGAIN

You will never know the depths of
Sadness you have erased from
My mind and heart.
Because in my darkest hours
You were so kind to me.

You put faith back into my soul
When there was none and
Made me believe in friendships again
And an angels work had been done.

The feathers you wore in your hair was
A sign from god to let me know that
He was here through his angel that
He sent to me, now I believe.

You asked him to use you and he did.
An unseen power guiding you and
You never knew your assignment was me.
Thank you God for sending her to me.
Now once again I believe.

BY:JESY

4-27-2012

ONLY YOU CAN LIGHT THE CANDLE TO MY HEART

Each time I remember those days of growing up;
When we were all at home
snuggled in the warmth of security.
Knowing you were always there for us kids and
Made sure we were all ok.
Even when there were times you could have
Chosen to be somewhere else.

We're all grown up now and you are still here for
Each one of us kids.
I wanted you to know how glad I am that you are.
There are no words that I could express to
Let you know that God gave me the greatest dad that
Anyone could ever want.
When he chose you to be my dad.

BY:JESY

OUR COUNTY FAIR

I went to the fair this year
The smell of cotton candy in the air.
The ferris wheel going around
Cups and debris on the ground.
The ticket booth and pony rides
Clear bowls with fish inside.
People everywhere walking here and there
You knew you was at the fair.

We went over to the barn
Where animals were in their pins
And fans blowing on them.
A hot July afternoon
Thinking don't worry
We'll be home soon.
All the rides you can see
And children lined up just like you and me.

Hot dog stands and waffle cakes

Pork chops and corn cobs on the grill.

And the roller coaster ride oh what a thrill.

Popping balloons and winning games.

I'll take the teddy bear on the top shelf

I heard the child say.

I thought to myself this has been a wonderful day.

BY:JESY

1-20-2012

OUR FINAL GOODBYE

We both knew it was a matter of time
When we would have to say our final goodbyes.
For your battle with cancer has come to an end.

You fought a long hard fight
For it was not in vain.
Every moment spent
Was one more precious memory you left behind.

I'll remember you as you were then
Laughing and having a good time
And these memories I'll hold closer to my heart.

And as I have rolled with these emotions
From my heart and mind
And not wanting to see you go.

I know that your suffering is over
And your soul is free
From the illness that laid within your body.

For it is now
that the time has come
That we have said our final goodbye.

BY:JESY
11-4-2012

OUR FISHING POND

It is a place where we go to forget about
Our troubles and woos.
Where we sometimes stay late into
The night waiting for the fish to bite.
While sitting there under the moonlight.

It is the catching of the big fish that
Gives you such a rush.
And the peacefulness of this place
That I love so much.
It is the time we spend together I love most of all.
We fish from the spring time clear into the fall.

We've met a few friends here that
Has lasted threw time.
While casting out our fishing poles and
Reeling in our line.
As we spend hours just talking to each other in
The serene place we call our second home.

BY:JESY
12-20-2011

OUR FRIEND

You've lived your life long and fulfilled,
Exciting and thrilled
By the stories you've told
As your memories began to unfold.

I listened for hours while sitting next to you
Of beautiful stories inside of you
And of a life I never knew.

You've taken my heart and mind to places
I've never been as I have traveled back
Into time where you had been; back then.

You've put smile's on my face and
tears in my eye's
As you have shared with me your life.

Today we will say goodbye to our
Friend so dear and of
Your stories we will no longer hear.

We will lay you to rest as we stand there and cry
For our friend no longer in our lives.
We'll miss you and all the things we used to do
Goodbye our friend: we love you.

BY:JESY
(Jeneil E. Sparks, Young)
10-6-2012

OUR MEMORY HOME

I went past the house we once called home
Just an empty field remains along with
The steps that led up to our memory home.

A place where our family built our memories
There for many years and as I sat there in a
Constant stare I pushed back the tears that
Flowed down my face for now this is just an
Empty space.

It has been many years since we lived there
And yet I still remember every room
And eleven years of memories now lie in its tomb.
As the thoughts come flowing back to me
Of those precious memories that will forever remain
In our memory home.

BY:JESY
2-8-2012

OUT OF THE BLUE

I thought of you again last night,
And all the things we used to do.
Your touch so sweet and tender.
Your words so soft and true.
Suddenly out of the blue.
I was reliving the memory of you.

It has been a long time now
Since you've passed away,
I've always held in my heart that dreadful day.
But it is the love you had for me
That gets me through each day.
Out of the blue the sadness left me
As I thought of the memory of you.

BY:JESY

PAPER WISHES

It is my dream of things
As I write them down on paper.
If only a fairy would wave her wand
And give me magical paper.
I would tare it in half
And give one to you.
Then all of our wishes could come true.

Paper wishes and ideas and things
That as for now
 is only of dreams.
I would make a list one, two three . . .
While thinking it through carefully.
I'd tell myself; don't be in a rush
And think of things that would
Make me blush.

Now I'd be selfish; I will not lie

Cause paper wishes are like

No limits in the sky.

Then I would calm myself down

I'd think of the things

That has made me frown.

Then to put a smile back upon my face

I would include

all of God's Glory and Grace

For this world we live in

And paper wishes to believe in.

BY:JESY

9-29-2012

SHATTERED

How can it be, you leaving me
As you stormed out the door
Saying you don't love me anymore.
That you found someone new
And that you love her too.

Shattered in an instant, and feeling all alone
And realizing your never coming home.
How can this be, you leaving me
For the first time, in my lifetime.

As the tear's flowed, this feeling I could not hide.
I was starting to feel a little crazy inside.
A feeling of all the lies and deceit, you did to me.
How can I go on, with a feeling of defeat.

Shattered in an instant and feeling all alone
And realizing your never coming home.
How can this be, you leaving me
For the second time, in my lifetime.

I picked my heart up off the floor

When there was a knock at the door

And all the sheriff could say

Was there was an accident

And I'm sorry lady

but your husband has passed away.

Shattered in an instant and feeling all alone.

And realizing your never coming home

How can this be, you leaving me

For the last time, in my lifetime.

By:JESY

9-27-2012

SHE IS I

She painted a picture today of you
By the words she spoke.
Put you on a pedestal with the
Poems she wrote; about you.
It all came from her heart and
She's loved you from the start.

She holds her vows so true to
Her husband that is you.
For all you do for her in her life
That's why she is so proud to be your wife
And in her soul; you've taken
Her frowns and turned them up side down.

You put a smile back upon her face and
Held her with a warm embrace and
As she thanks God for you
She'll always know the reasons why
Because she is I.

BY:JESY
4-27-2012

SISTER'S ARE FOREVER

I have begun to reflect upon my life
Remembering you, the struggles and strife's
I'm beginning to see you in a different light.
As I see our paths are so much alike.
We have began to be the best of friends
As our relationship is on the mend.

I can see now how much you mean to me
And without you I wouldn't be me
And in my heart is where you will always be.
A sacred place for you and me.
For I know now the older I get
You're the one my heart will never forget.

I know things will be just fine
As we share emotions yours and mine
Forever we will be sisters you and me
And life long friends you will see.
Two worlds we now can share and
Always know I'll be there.
Until our lives shall end
You are my sister, my best friend.

BY: JESY
7-26-2012

THE BEAUTY OF IT ALL

Marriage to me:
Is the sharing of two souls
Joined together by love and emotions
That runs deeper than the ocean
Of glitter and gold to have and to hold
For a lifetime.

A vow to take:
Two people to never forsake
Like diamond rings
And glamorous things.
Two hearts that becomes one
Until our lives are done.

An oath we make:
The journey we will take
Two people joined together by fate
And for life we will mate.
As we catch each other when we fall
These are the things
That is the beauty of it all.

BY:JESY
7-13-2012

THE BIGGER SIDE OF ME

I was laughed at, teased and called
All kinds of names.
I've lived my life in turmoil and shame.
I didn't want anyone to know
what was hurting deep inside of me.
So I covered it up with denial
That caused my weight to go in a
Upward spiral.
And all you could see
Was the bigger side of me.

I wanted to stop eating so much
But it was the only comfort I could find
In a world of sadness
I wanted to leave behind.
I put myself through more hell
That did not need to be.
And all you could see
Was the bigger side of me.

The years of suppressed memories
Are what put these pounds on me
If only I could have seen
What this was doing to me.
I have no one to blame but me
For my demise
So I've dealt with some emotions
To lower my size.

100 pounds has came off of me
A whole other person you no longer see.
Because now I'm dealing with these
Suppressed memories.
And one day you will no longer see
The bigger side of me.

By:JESY
9-28-2012

THE BIRD'S

As I sit here watching the birds
Gathering on the telephone line.
I'm hearing them chirp in a language
Unknown to mine.
The beauty of there hovering wings
Fills my mind with peaceful things

Then flying off into the trees
Are flock's of birds landing on its leaves.
Then one by one I see them fly over
To the bird feeder shoulder to shoulder.
So many wanting to eat all at once
As they all begin to launch.
Then I feel a smile coming over me
And a feeling of being free.

There gathered on the ground are many too
The bird above kicking out seeds for them too.
Such a precious sight nature has givin me
A peace from heaven we all can see.
And here before me I see threw my eyes
The beauty of the birds in the skys.

BY: JESY

9-2-2012

58

THE BULLY

There is no place in my heart for you
Each time you do what you do
And even when you've been unkind
I forgave you in my mind.
I won't forget the wrong you have done
But letting it go I feel I've won.
Its freed me from the hold
You have had on my thoughts.

I no longer let you disturb my emotions
Just because you had the notion
To be mean to me.
You claim it's all in fun
I say it isn't when it's my feelings being done
And used in a negative way.
I've only got one thing to say
SHAME ON YOU GO AWAY!

BY: JESY
1-9-2012

THE GUARDIAN TREE

How could I have not noticed before
When for many years you have stood
Outside my door.

This old tree that has shaded me
Has a face in it so amazing to see.
I call it the guardian tree.

A tree of age hundreds of years
The man of this tree he has a beard
Bushy eye brows, a nose, eyes and mouth
His face stern, his body stout.

Sometimes I wonder
Has nature been watching over me
With this old mans face in the tree.

Forever more facing my door
Stands natures beauty to see
Is this old tree watching over me.

BY:JESY

12-10-2012

THE LAST HUG

I'll never forget you
As you are laid to rest.
The hugs you gave me
Were the best.
As I say goodbye to you
My friend.
I didn't know our last hug
Would be the end.

I'll carry with me these
Hugs so dear.
And in my heart
They'll see me through
Each year.
As you have touched my life
With sweet memories of you.
Your in heaven now
To hug the angels
Like we used to do.

I'll never forget you
For in my heart
I can truly say
The last hug will forever stay
As a reminder of a man so kind
To this heart of mine.

By: JESY
7-26-2012

THE LOVE INSIDE OF ME

The love inside of me
Is for a God we can not see.
He gave his only begotten son.
To forgive the sins we have done.

The love inside of me
Is for a man whom first believed
Took a seed and breathed life into me
And will hold me in his heart for eternity.

For carrying me through troublesome times
In this world of yours and mine.
I'll tell the world how great he is
For the unconditional love he gives.

The love inside of me
Is for a God we can not see.
He gave his only begotten son.
To forgive the sins we have done.

BY: JESY
2-6-2013

THE LULLABY

I remember the humming lullaby
You used to hum to me
When I was just a baby
And ever now and then
I'll hum it again
Just to feel you next to me
Because I love you mommy.

Even though you are in heaven now
I'll always have the lullaby
You hummed to me.
A treasure you left me years ago
I still carry with me.
A priceless treasure I know will
Never leave my soul
Because I miss you mommy.

BY:JESY
5-6-2012

THE MOST BEAUTIFUL THING

The most beautiful thing
I've ever seen
Is the love in his eyes
As a man holds his baby
For the first time.

The most beautiful thing
I've ever seen
Is the compassion on her face
As her friend has fallin from grace.

The most beautiful thing
I've ever seen
Is someone reaching out
And giving a helping hand.

And the most beautiful thing
I've ever seen
Is the look in your eyes
As you told me you loved me
Last night.

By:JESY
9-27-2012

THE SEED

God planted a seed years ago
In my mothers womb
And as he watched it grow
My mother came to know
She was carrying a baby within.

And in the time until I was born
The story of my life was written; with no pages torn.
He gave me gifts instilled in me for his plan.
He chose the day and I was born and my life began.

There is so much more to this story you will see
And all you have to do is believe.
Yes there will be hard times to make you grow
And sad times to help you know
A love so deep within that it all began with him.

The dreams you have inside; never let them go
For one day you will know
The full circle of his plan
You are here for a reason you must understand
For you are the seed for Gods plan.

BY:JESY

10-15-2012

THE SHADOW'S

Standing in the shadows of your light
Piercing the darkness just to grasp the light
For you are within my reach.

I've fallin behind in my dreams
Of uncertainty's, ideas and things
And the strength I have inside
To never let it go.
Then victory will be mine
And out of the shadows I will climb.

There is a passion deep within my soul
For this dream of mine to come alive
And a legacy to leave behind
with a love so deep within
That will carry me through until the end.

BY:JESY
11-7-2012

THE WALK HE THOUGHT
HE TOOK ALONE

Everyday I would see this homeless man go by with his
Friend at his side.
Pushing a cart with everything he owned inside.
It saddened me deep within my soul and I had to know.
God how could he have no home?

So one day I said hello and he said hi
I said I was just wondering why?
He said I have no home, no place to call my own and
Everyday I walk these streets alone.

So I asked him about his friend he said it was just him.
And as the tears fell from my eyes
There was something I realized.
The walk he thought he walked alone
Must have been with the man that rolled away the stone.

BY:JESY

4-11-2012

THIS CHRISTMAS

Oh how my heart has ached; even still
As the memories still feel so real.
I know in my heart it will never be like it was back then,
When you were here.
As I could never forget you dear.

It's Christmas time again and another year gone by
That the empty chair at the table will not be filled
With you in it and
No presents under the tree with your name on it.
If only we could have had one more Christmas dinner,
Just one more holiday with you.

Well this year I'll try to do everything I can
So the memories will not come flooding through.
I'll try to chase away the sadness that
Tares my heart in two
And make the best of this Christmas without you.

BY:JESY

12-24-2011

# TIMELINE

As I sit here looking in the mirror
I find myself drifting back into the past.
The memories of this life has held
Are timelessly scattered.
In the universe of my mind stories that
Unfolded through the years.

For there are people I've met some
I have yet to forget others
That have faded into the
Forgotten world in my mind.
For the loves, the dreams and
The melodies reminded only by a song or
Vision gone by.

And then there is the memory of
The pain that I've endured the sorrows I've
Had trapped in a lifetime I couldn't let go of.
So I sit here before the mirror and see
The ageing years upon my face and
Realize threw it all I am still beautiful to me.

BY:JESY
DEC. 3, 2011

# VACATION

I'm taking a vacation the only kind I can afford.
I'm going to a place I've never been before.
So I'll turn my computer on and
I'll look up airplanes, beaches and more
I'll also look up museums and
Pretend I'm going on a tour.

As I sit at my computer desk wasting time.
Going on this vacation in my mind.
I'm sure your thinking by now I'm just not right
As I tell you I'm leaving on a plane tonight.
So for a little while no one disturb me please.
I'm on vacation as I jokingly tease.

BY:JESY

1-10-2012

WEED'S

The place you called imperfect to you.
Was perfect to me.
It was my sacred garden you see.
A place I could go and find my peace
To cry and release.

You took out some flowers and weeds
Placed what you wanted in it
And called it your own.
Since you destroyed it for me
I gave it to you and let it be.

What was is now gone
So I made a new one.
Yes it will take awhile to get it right again
And I won't disown you my friend.
Just next time ask first of all
Because it wasn't yours at all.

Thank you for the help you thought
You were giving me.
Something's are sacred even the weeds.
For they mean to me the ending of a
Life once lived
And the withering of beauty
They did give.

BY:JESY
5-12-2012

YOU ARE THERE

I can see you standing there
In the mist, in the air
You are there, you are there

I find myself in the clouds
I hear a voice it speaks out loud
You are there, you are there

And in the midst of the night
I can see your guiding light

I can see in the air
All that I can find is there
It is you
You are there, you are there

And in my heart I will always know
A peacefulness only you can show
You are there, you are there
You have always been there

BY:JESY
1-8-2013